DAVID FOSTER
ELEVEN WORDS

ISBN 978-1-5400-8406-4

For all works contained herein:
Unauthorized copying, arranging, adapting, recording, Internet posting, public performance,
or other distribution of the music in this publication is an infringement of copyright.
Infringers are liable under the law.

Visit Hal Leonard Online at
www.halleonard.com

Contact us:
Hal Leonard
7777 West Bluemound Road
Milwaukee, WI 53213
Email: info@halleonard.com

In Europe, contact:
Hal Leonard Europe Limited
42 Wigmore Street
Marylebone, London, W1U 2RN
Email: info@halleonardeurope.com

In Australia, contact:
Hal Leonard Australia Pty. Ltd.
4 Lentara Court
Cheltenham, Victoria, 3192 Australia
Email: info@halleonard.com.au

EVERLASTING

By DAVID FOSTER

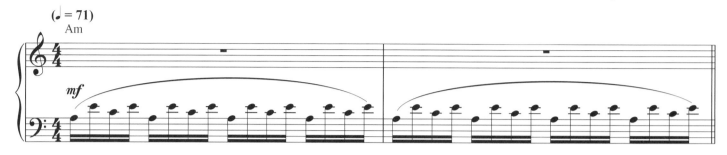

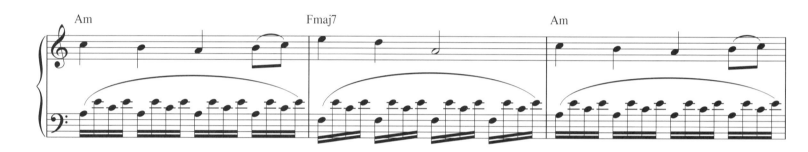

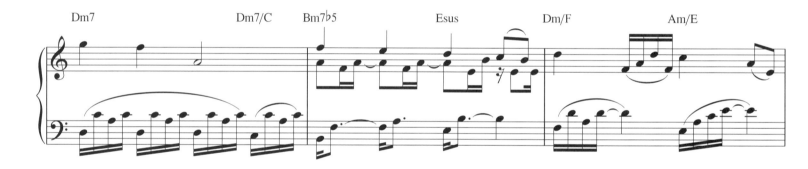

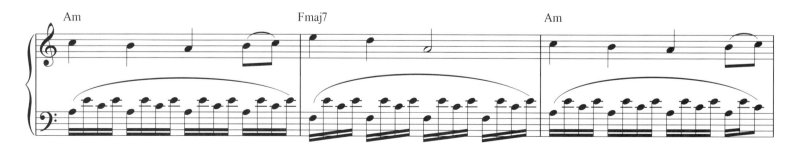

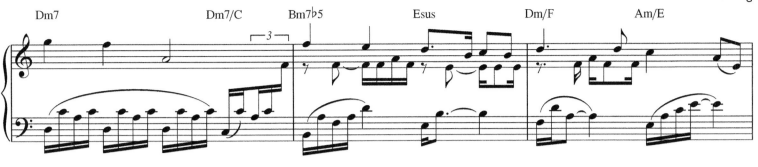

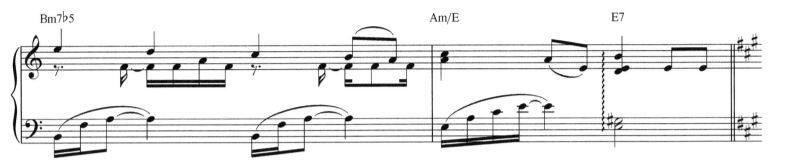

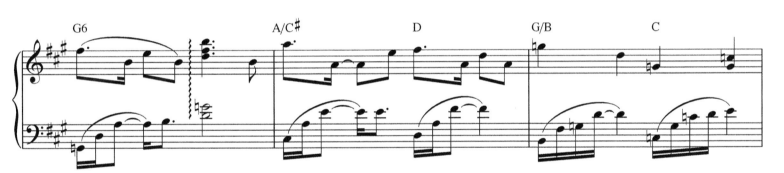

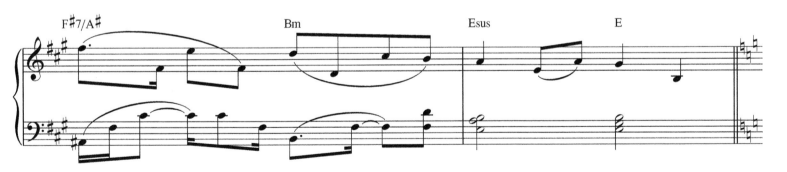

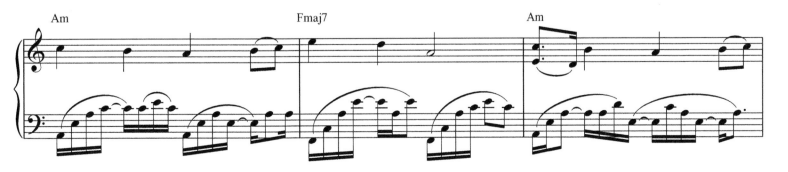

4

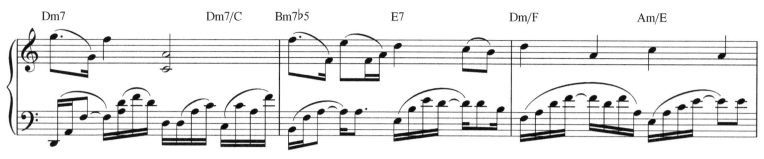

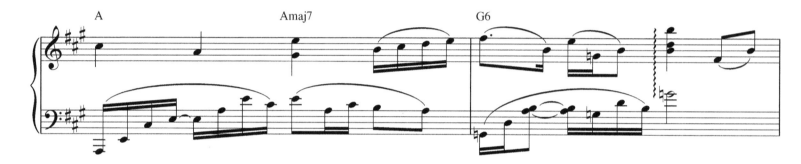

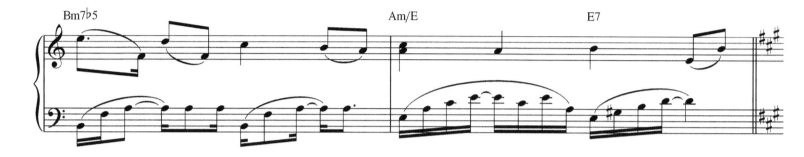

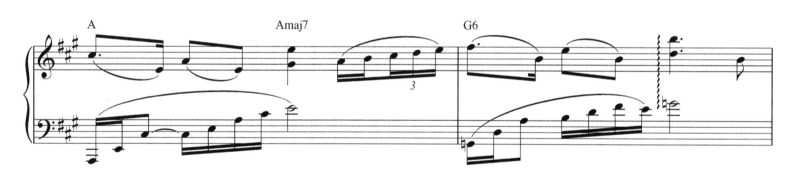

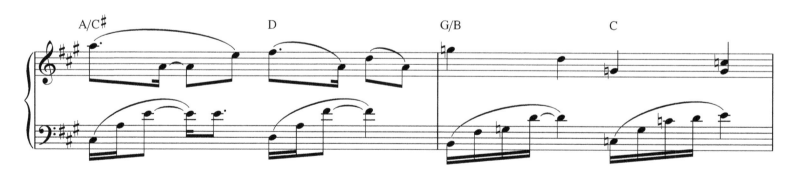

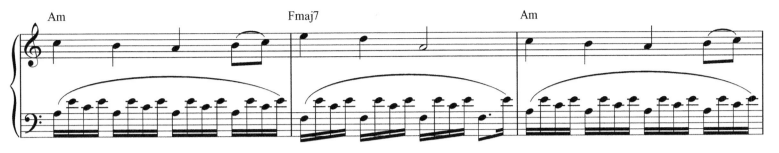

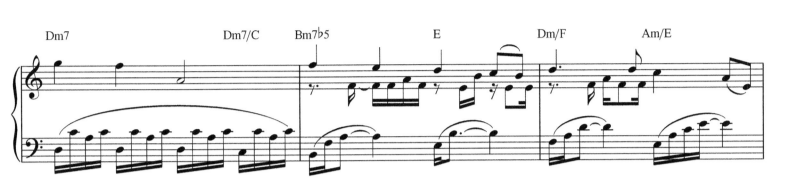

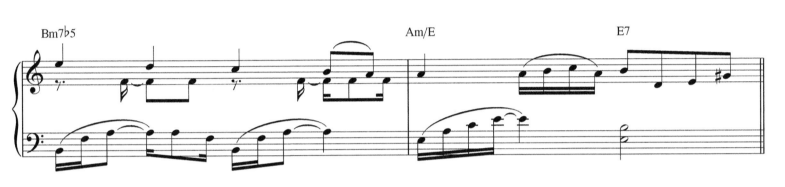

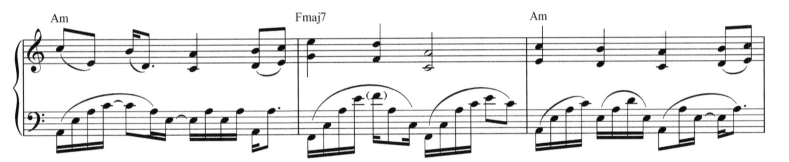

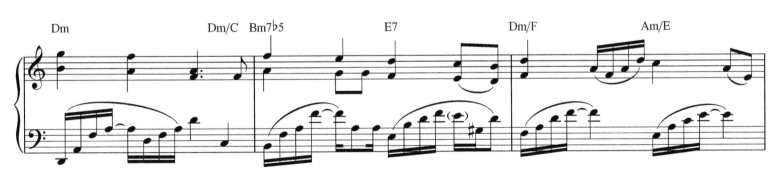

LOVE

By DAVID FOSTER

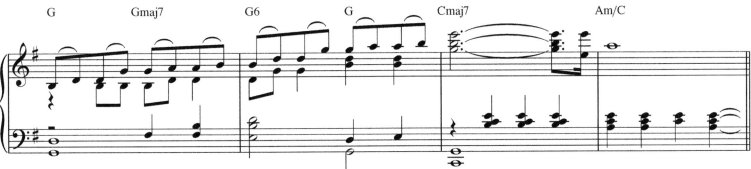

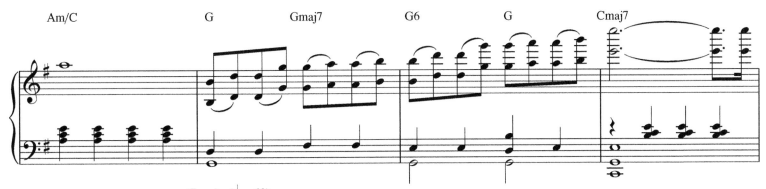

ETERNITY

By JIN JIE LIN

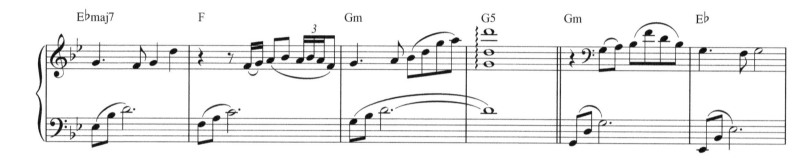

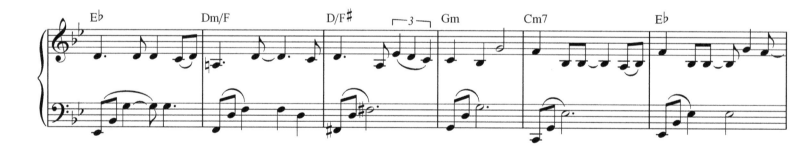

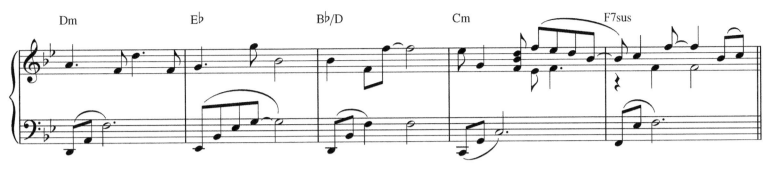

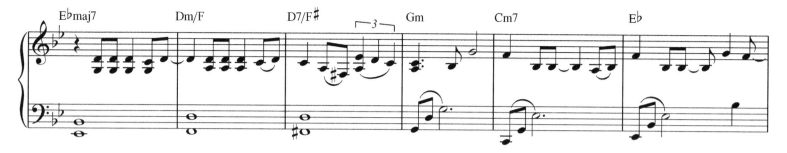

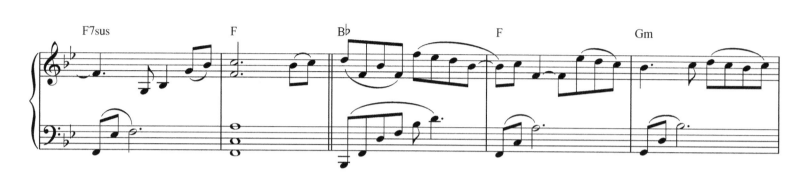

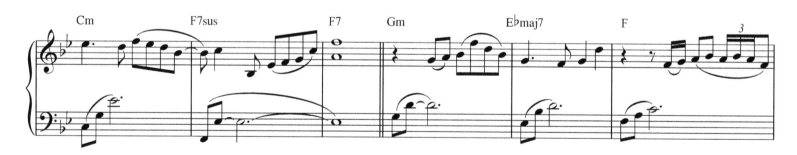

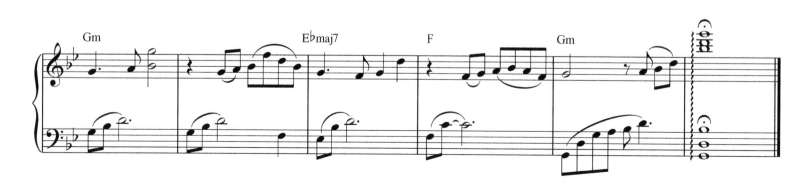

WONDERMENT

By DAVID FOSTER

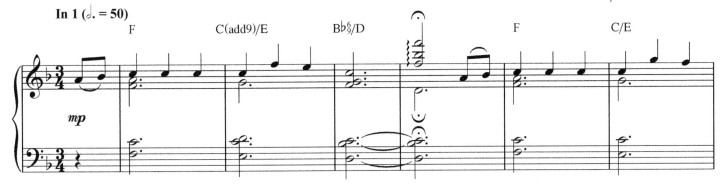

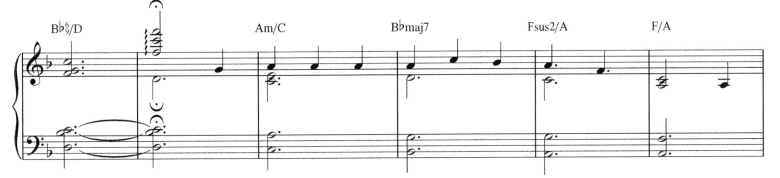

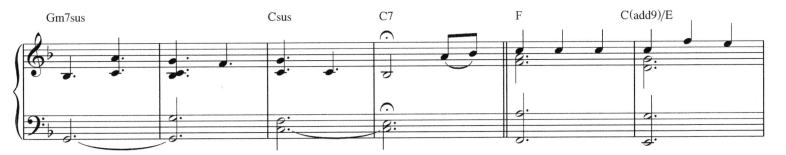

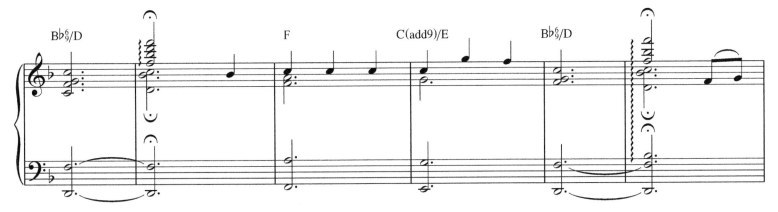

12

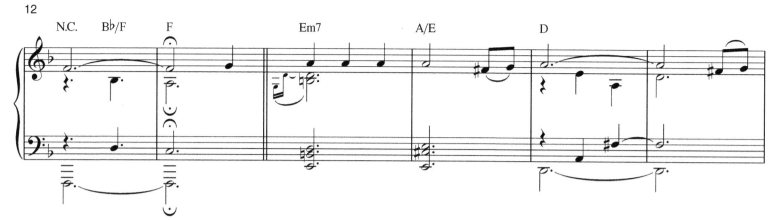

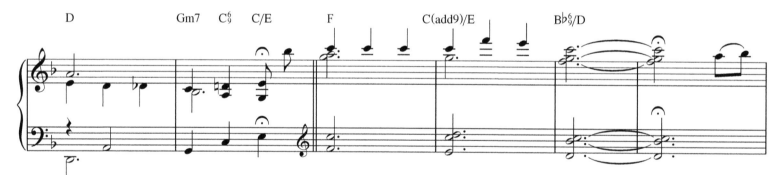

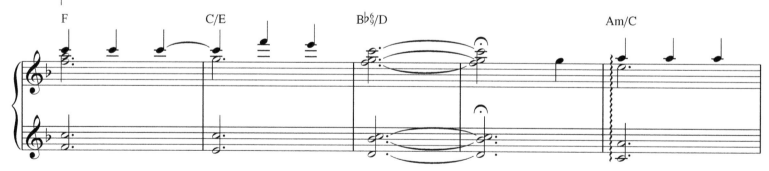

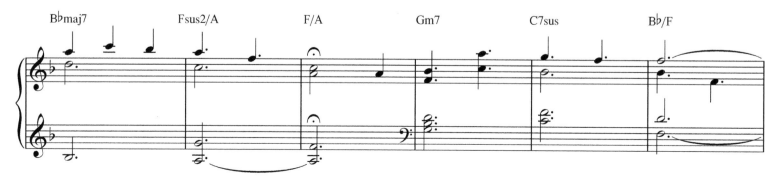

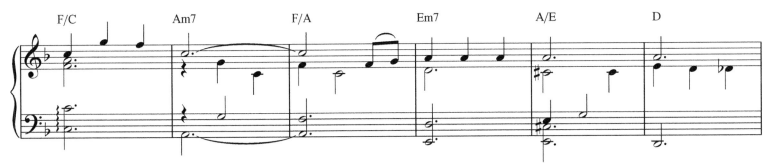

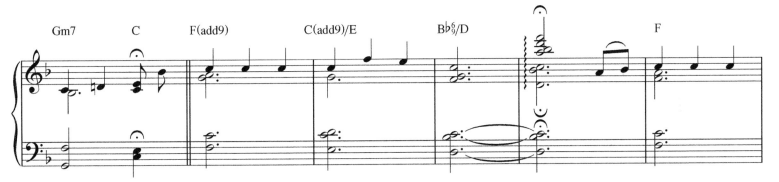

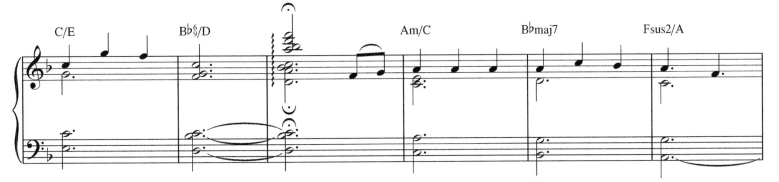

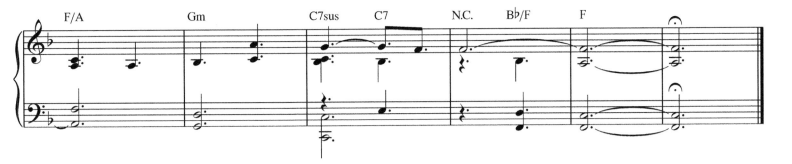

VICTORIOUS

By DAVID FOSTER

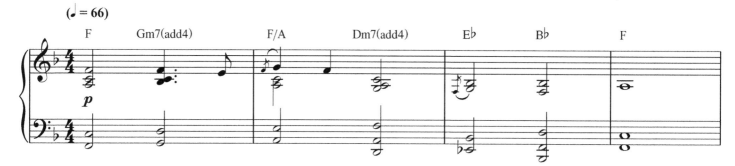

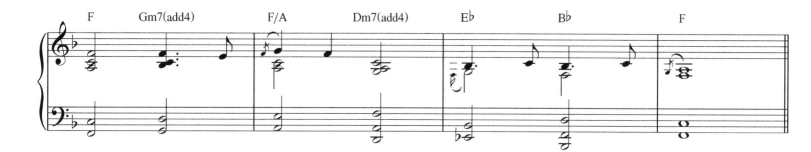

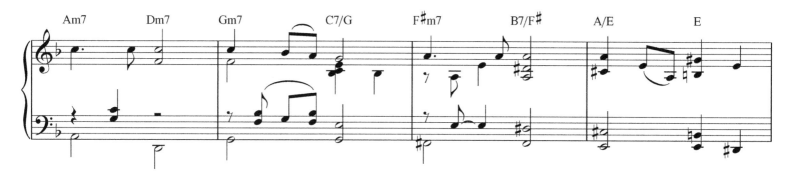

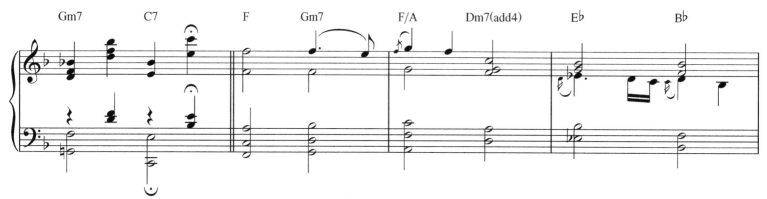

15

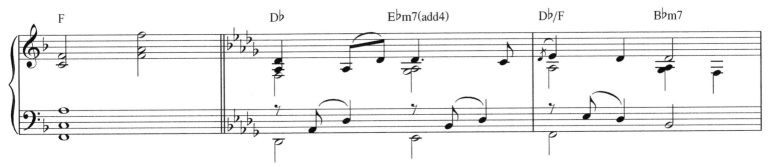

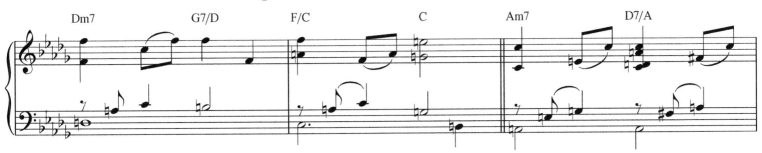

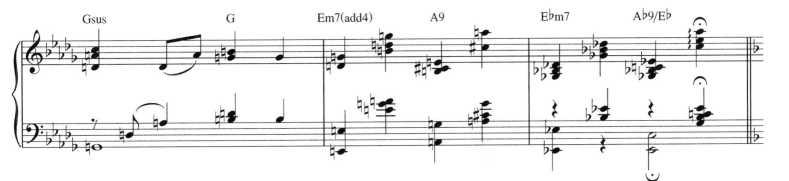

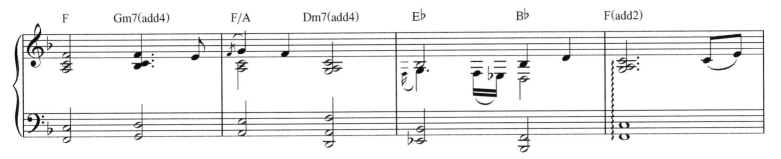

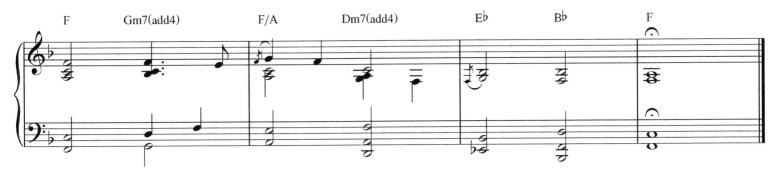

ELEGANT

By DAVID FOSTER

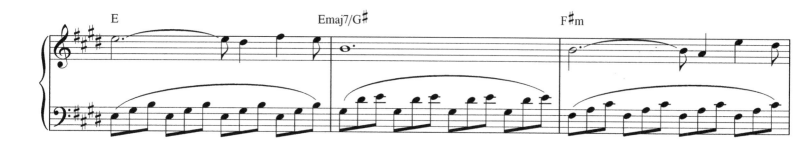

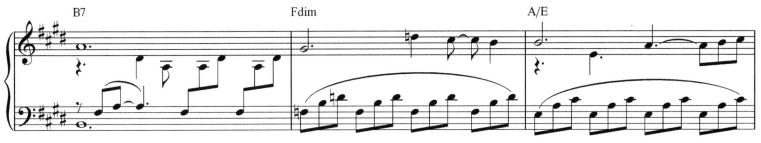

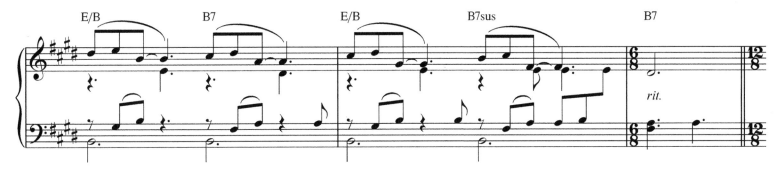

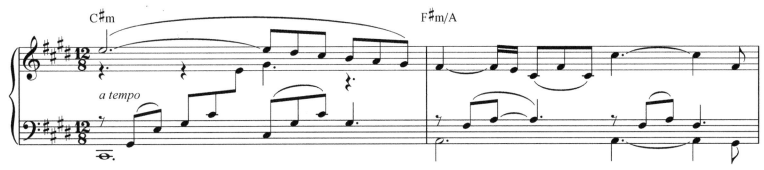

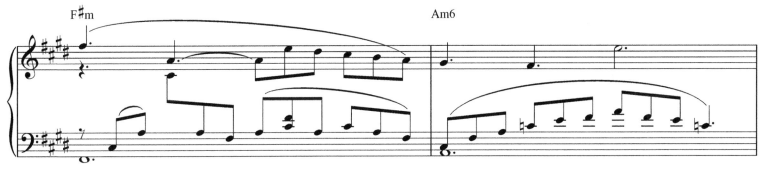

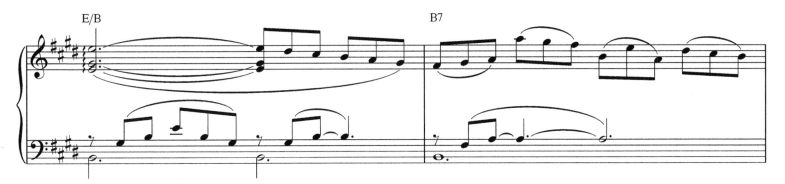

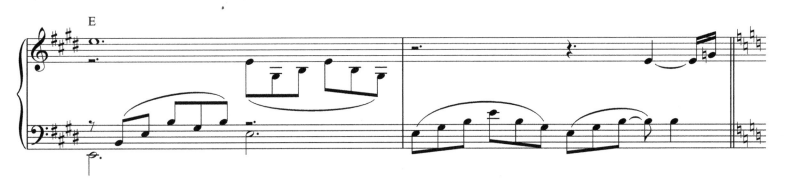

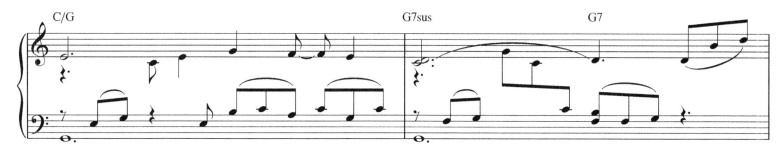

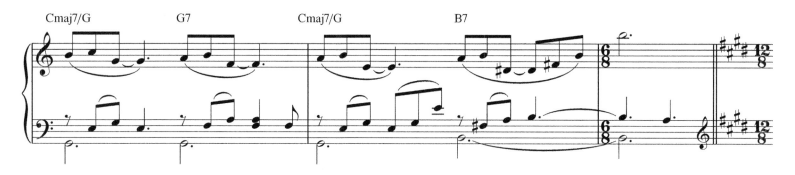

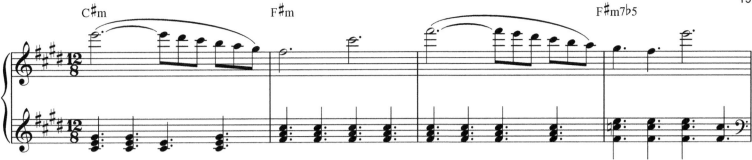

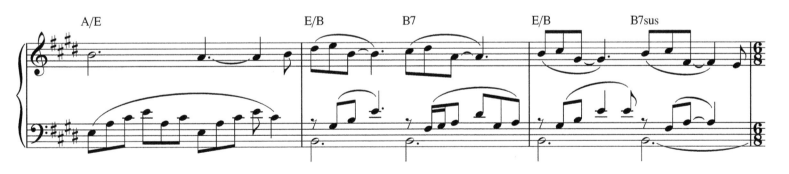

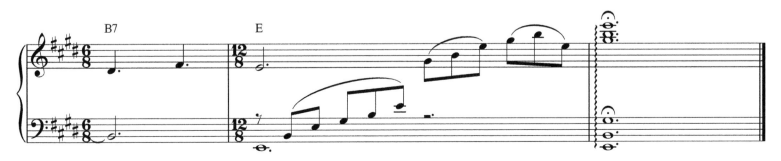

NOBILITY

By DAVID FOSTER

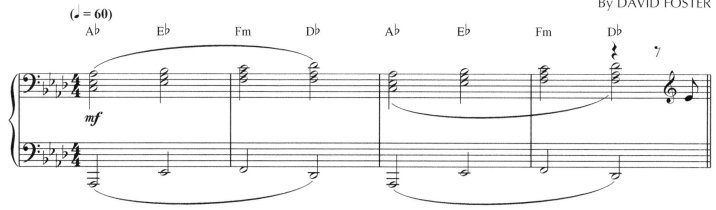

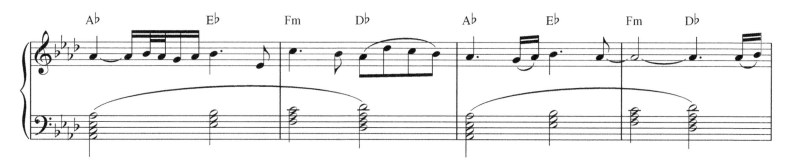

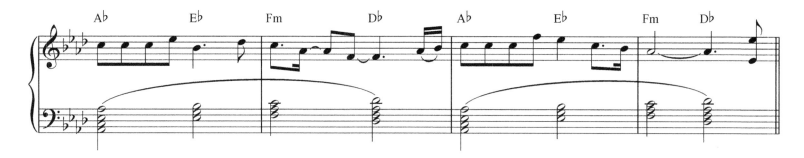

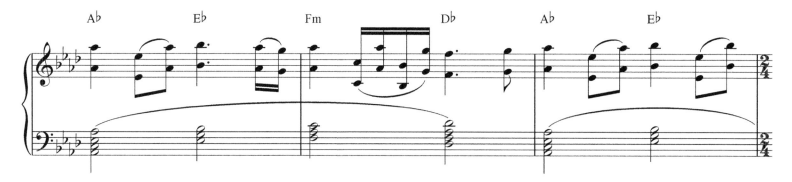

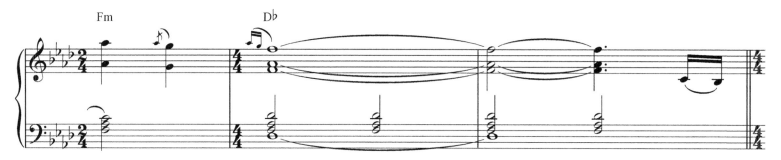

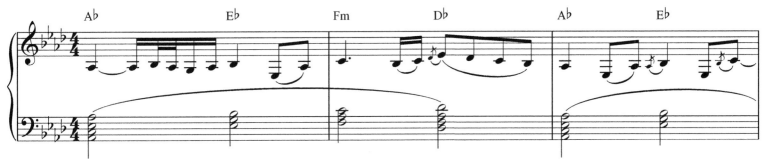

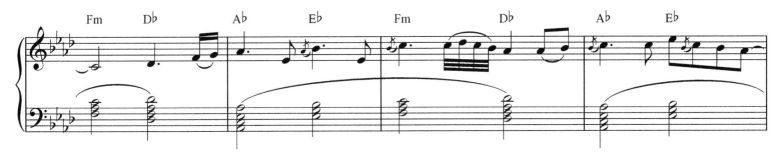

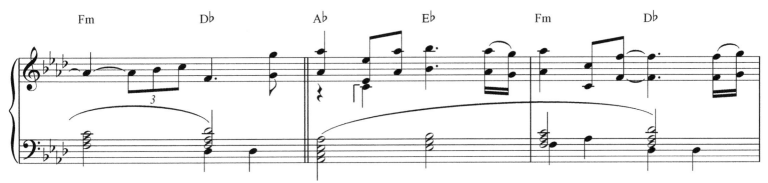

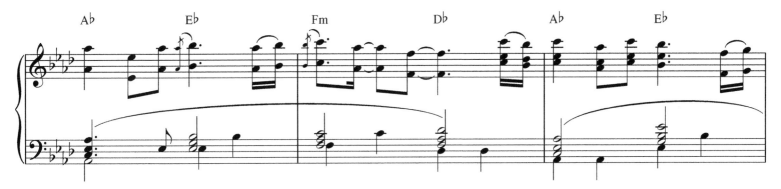

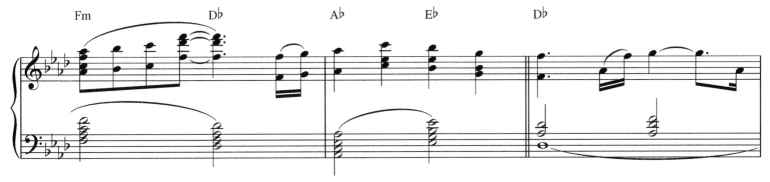

ORBITING

By DAVID FOSTER

Slow Waltz (♩ = 106)

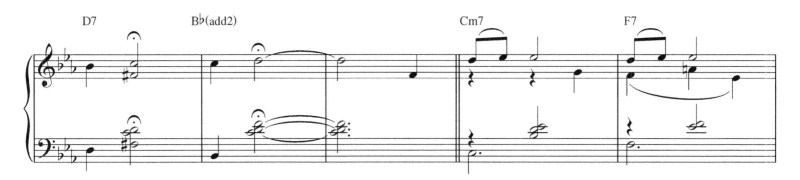

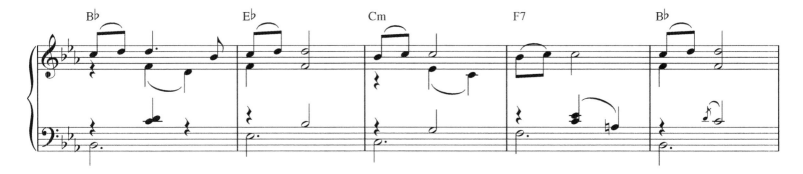

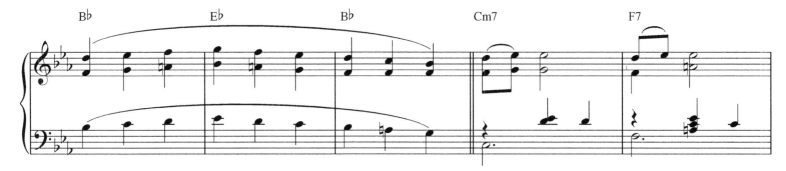

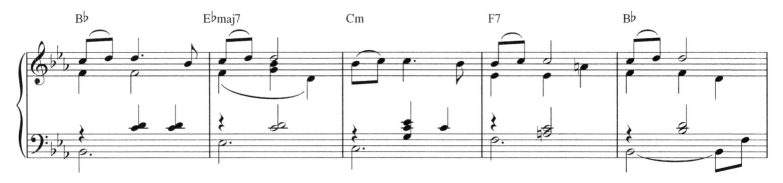

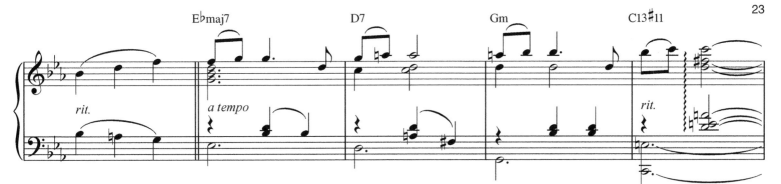

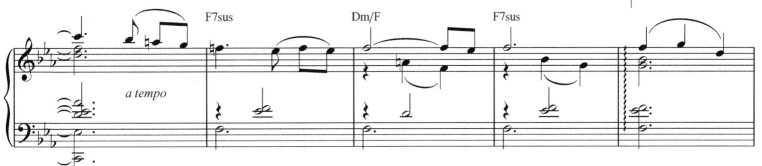

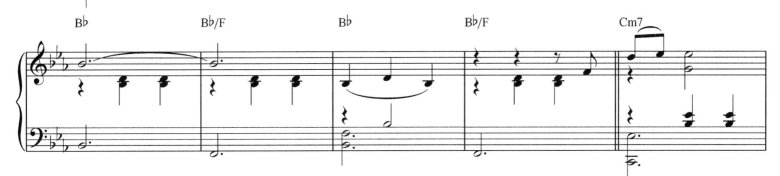

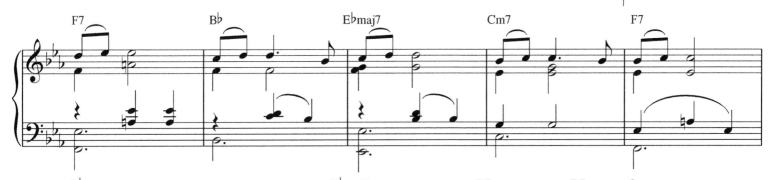

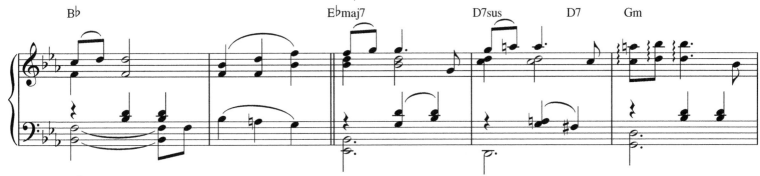

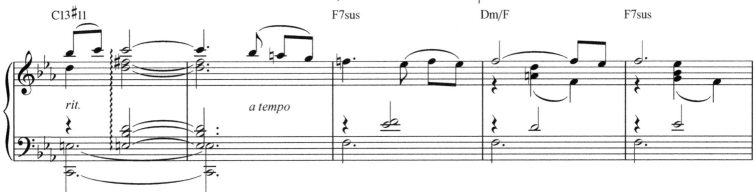

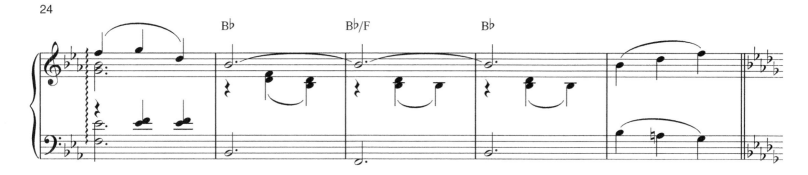

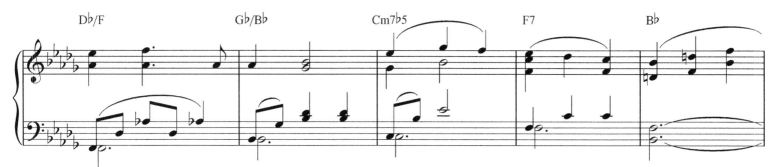

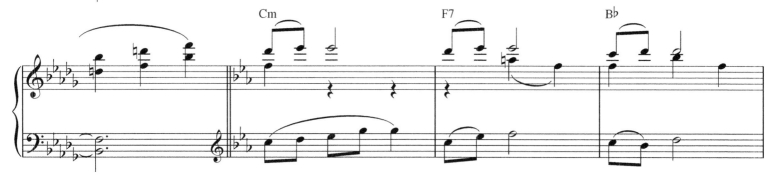

ROMANCE

Traditional Chinese Children's Song
Arranged by DAVID FOSTER

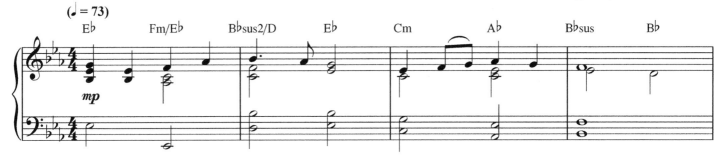

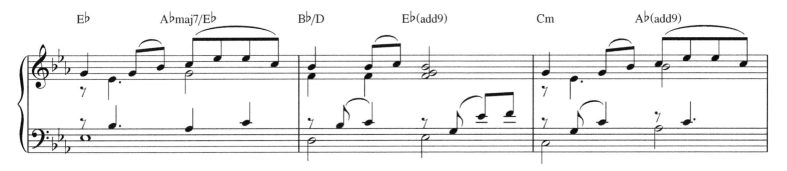

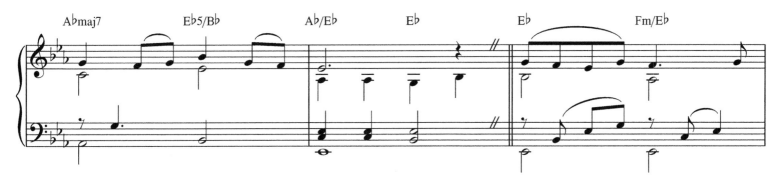

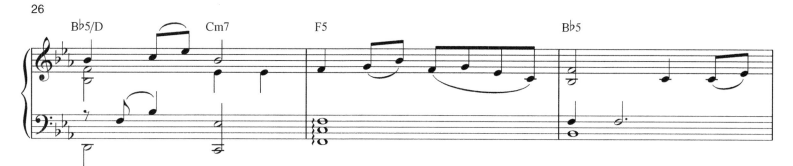

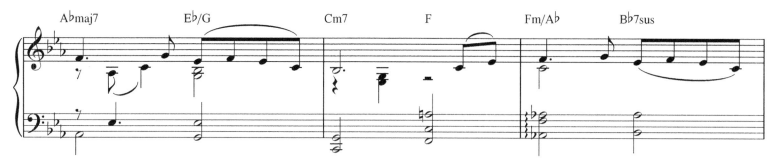

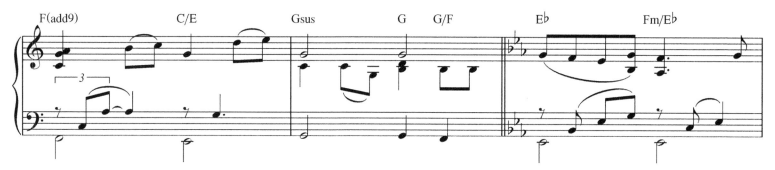

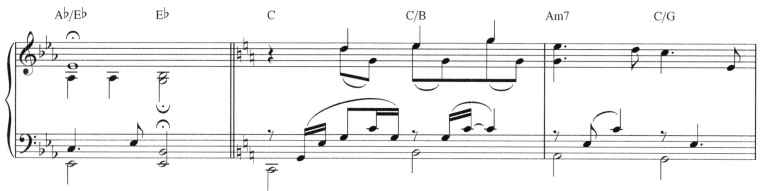

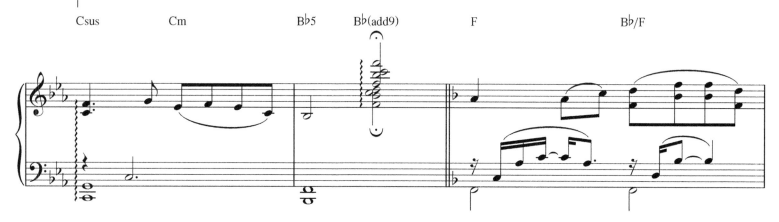

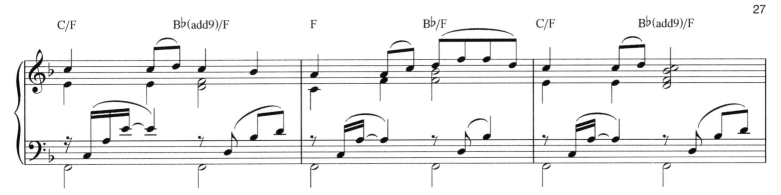

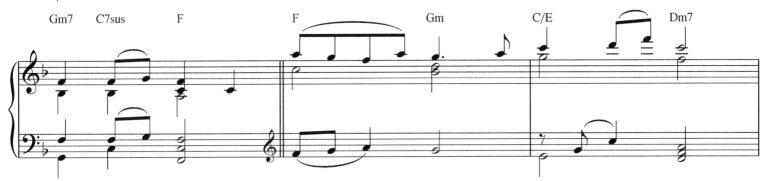

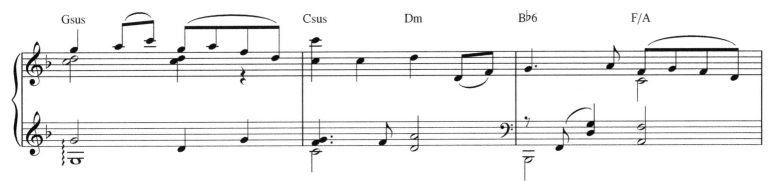

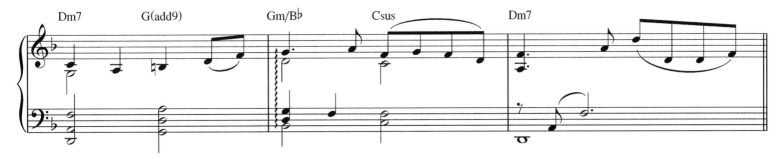

SERENITY

By DAVID FOSTER

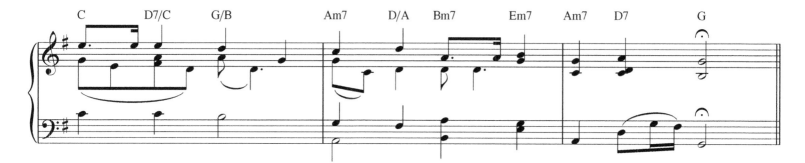

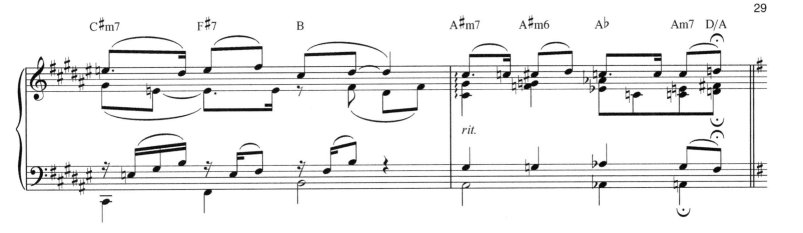

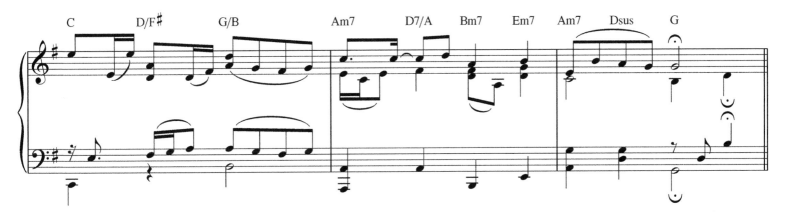

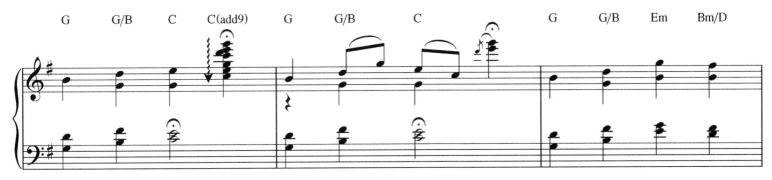

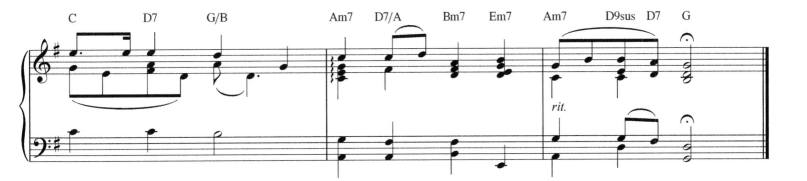

DREAMS

By DAVID FOSTER

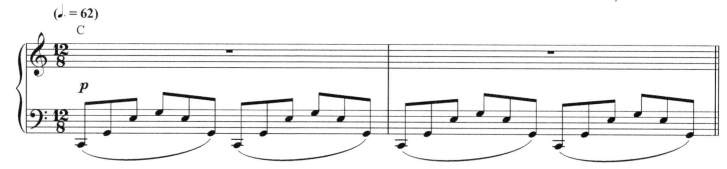

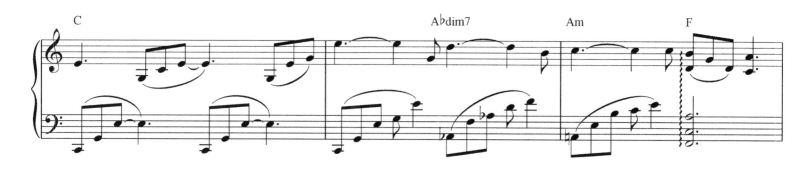

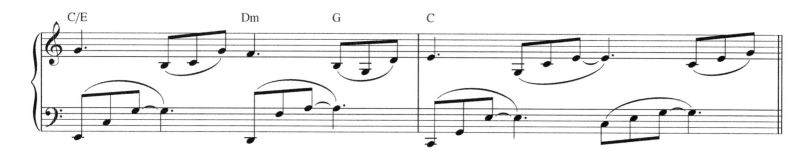

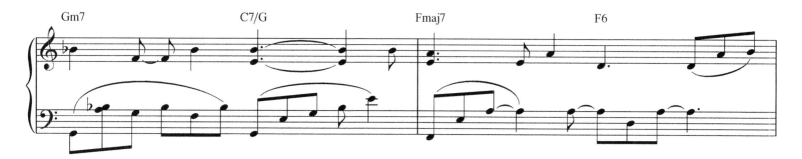

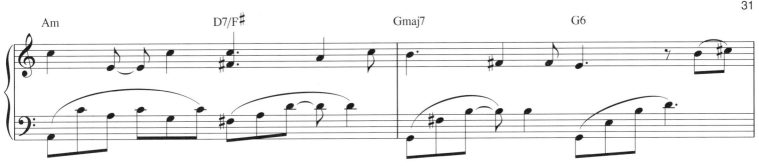

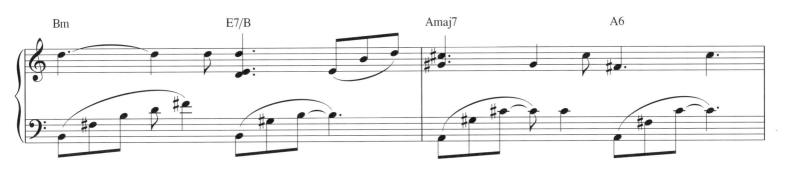

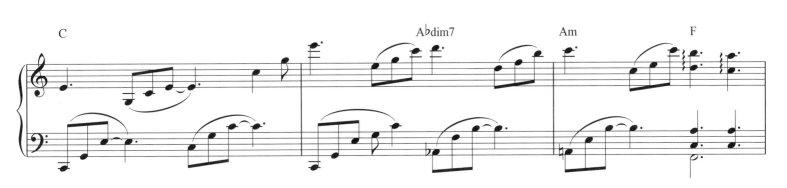

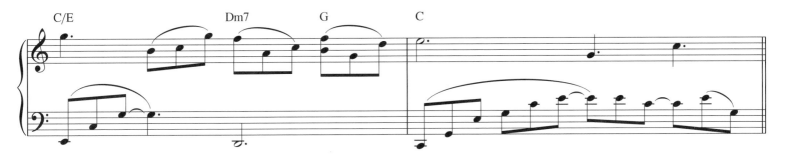

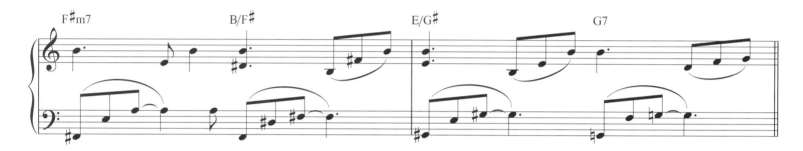

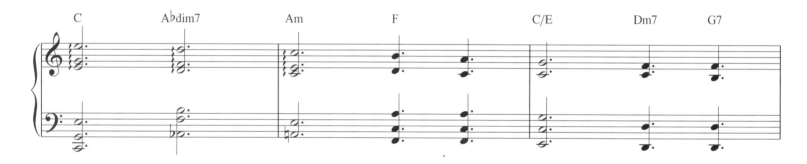

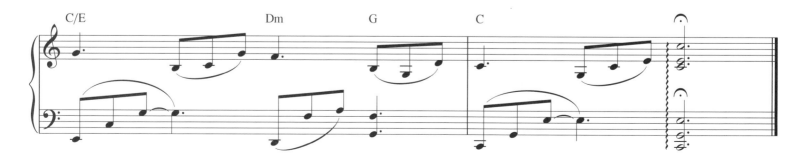